Enough

An Imperfect Antidote to Perfectionism

By
Vix Anderton

www.vixanderton.com

Copyright © 2022 Vix Anderton

All rights reserved. No part of this book may be reproduced or distributed in any form without prior written permission from the author, with the exception of non-commercial uses permitted by copyright law.

Cover Image by Nathalie Alburjas www.utterlycreate.com

CONTENTS

Introduction	1
Perfectionism Isn't About Trying to be Perfect	5
An Antidote to Perfectionism	11
Five Flavours of Perfectionism	17
How You Do One Thing Is How You Do Everything	25
Perfectionism Is a Lonely Game	29
Being Busy Keeps Us Safe	33
This Road Leads to Burnout	37
A Way to Radical Self-Acceptance	45
The Dance Between Self-Acceptance, Self-Improvement and Never Being Good Enough	49
It's Not *The Thing*, It's Your Relationship To *The Thing*	53
The Power of Appreciation	57
Stop Trying So Hard	61
Authenticity Over Perfection	67
What Self-Care Really Means	71
Conclusion: Doing Perfectionist While Writing a Book About Perfectionism	77
Acknowledgements	83
About The Author	85

Introduction

For as long as I can remember, I've been a perfectionist.

I came home aged 6, totally inconsolable after I didn't understand something at school. My teacher had mentioned something in a biology lesson that's usually taught to children 3 years older and I was sure there was something wrong with me because I hadn't understood. I didn't say anything at the time; I didn't ask a question. I simply assumed that my teacher expected me to understand (because why else would she say it) and I was a failure because I didn't get it. This incident is the encapsulation of my experience as a perfectionist: the deep pain I felt because I wasn't good enough. I wish I could tell you how I felt at that moment but I can't. I have no recollection of this; it's become one of those stories my mum tells because it's so me. I imagine you have your own version of this – getting hot and flustered somewhere, because you don't understand or it's not working, and being seemingly incapable of asking for the help you need.

The funny thing is that I didn't really know I was a perfectionist. Perfectionism was so deeply ingrained in me that it didn't even occur to me that I could live any other way. Almost the opposite, in fact. "I'm a bit of a perfectionist" would be my answer to that awkward interview question about what my weaknesses were, as some kind of humble-brag.

We live in a world that conditions us for perfectionism. So many attributes of perfectionism – like a relentless drive for improvement - are considered desirable, even as they erode our health and our sense of self-worth on the road to overwhelm and burnout.

It was only when I nearly burned out for the second time in two years that I even entertained an alternative to my always-on, always striving, never quite good enough way of being. This pattern of repeated episodes of burnout is common in the perfectionists I speak to and it doesn't surprise me that we never quite learn the lessons – the entire self-help industry is geared around seeing normal aspects of being human as a problem to fix along our road to enlightenment.

My early experiments with overcoming perfectionism set me up to see perfectionism as a character flaw. It was another sign that I was broken and that everything would be better if only I could fix myself. Yet no matter how hard I tried, I kept coming up against the same patterns. Wherever I went, there I was.

More through accident than by design, I found myself in the world of embodiment, initially through Authentic Relating.[1] I hadn't explicitly been searching for something to help my per-

---

[1] One definition of embodiment is becoming conscious of our usually unconscious personal shaping, developing a range of options in this regard, and having the freedom of choice as a result

fectionism and the practices I discovered proved to be my pathway to wholeness. I learnt to feel again; perfectionism had made me rigid and numb. And I started to uncover a way of being with my perfectionism that created deep, lasting change in my life.

As I've dived deeper into this world, my learnings inevitably started to transfer to my work as a coach and facilitator. I started to see how many of my clients were dealing with some form of perfectionism and I began sharing and teaching what I was learning through my training and my own journey.

This isn't a straightforward or easy journey. I still experience episodes when my perfectionist tendencies are in full swing, like in the writing of this very book. But those episodes are fewer and further apart. They've become more subtle and more manageable as I've developed more awareness of those patterns and more tools to help me make different choices so those perfectionist patterns are less likely to hold me back or keep me stuck.

And I hope that this book might help you start to do the same.

There is no magic formula to rid yourself of perfectionism. In fact, it's my assertion that you can't simply stop being a perfectionist. Perfectionism is a part of you, one that has no doubt been of service to you. If you're reading this, you might have started to realise that it also has a dark side that is preventing you from living the whole and rich life you desire.

What I hope to do in this book is offer an alternative perspective on perfectionism. One where you don't need to stop being a perfectionist because you are good enough as you are. You are not broken, you don't need fixing; you're human. This book is about awareness and choices. You'll discover how to redesign your relationship with perfectionism so that you can choose to put down the armour and be fully you in the world.

With grace and gratitude,

vix anderton

Perfectionism Isn't About Trying to be Perfect

*"Perfectionism doesn't make you feel perfect.
It makes you feel inadequate."*
~ Maria Shriver

Perfectionism is a misnomer.

Conventionally, perfectionism is defined as "a broad and multifaceted personality construct that involves the requirement of perfection or the appearance of perfection for the self or for others."[2]

But perfectionism isn't about trying to be perfect. It's the nagging feeling of never being good enough, of always being wrong.

So, if it's not about trying to be perfect, what is perfectionism?

Perfectionism is...

I can't talk about a definition of perfectionism without referencing the queen of shame and vulnerability, Brené Brown (from her books *The Gifts of Imperfection* and *Daring Greatly*).

---

[2] The *Corsini Encyclopaedia of Psychology (Volume 3)*, Hewitt and Flett

Here are her definitions of perfectionism:

1. Perfectionism is a **self-destructive** and **addictive** belief system that fuels this primary thought: *If I look perfect and do everything perfectly, I can avoid or minimise the painful feelings of blame, judgement, and shame.*
2. Perfectionism is an **unattainable** goal. We want to be perceived as perfect and there's no way to control perception, no matter how much time and energy is spent trying.
3. Perfectionism is **addictive**, because when we invariably do experience shame, judgement and blame, we often believe it's because we weren't perfect enough. Rather than questioning the **faulty logic** of perfectionism, we become even more entrenched in our quest to look and do everything just right.
4. Perfectionism is a defensive move. It's the belief that if we can do things perfectly and look perfect, we can minimise or avoid the pain of blame, judgement, and shame. Perfectionism is **a twenty-ton shield** that we lug around, thinking it will protect us, when in fact it's the thing that's preventing us from being seen.
5. Perfectionism sets us up to feel **more** shame, judgement and blame: *It's my fault. I'm feeling this way because I'm not good enough.*

Perfectionism, quite frankly, is exhausting!

Perfectionism takes away the joy of our adventurous spirit and dismisses our creative fun-loving selves.

That immensity of self-vigilance and control sucks up so much energy that it's hard to have enough left over for creation or love. Perfectionism kills ease and spontaneity. There's no flow with the deadweight of perfectionism.

Perfectionism chokes off our life force. Instead of channelling energy into the natural creativity of life, we end up chasing our tails in an endless mission to suppress everything, including our own selves, that's viewed as not good enough. It's the never-ending pursuit of better.

Perfectionism is a wall of fear that we hide behind, lest someone reject us and our imperfections. We present a sanitised, edited version of ourselves that we deem socially acceptable, all the while suppressing our authentic essence in case we're not good enough. Perfectionism can therefore feel safe, but that safety is an illusion, and the price for that false sense of security is real intimacy.

Ultimately, perfectionism is an exquisite form of self-torture and self-brutalisation. We demand constant improvement, always on the hunt for the next rush of self-development so we can temporarily feel complete. We bully ourselves into achieving; perfectionism is a relentless task-master, driving us to burnout.

And it's sneaky. Just when you think you've got a handle on it, it rears its head again with a whole new disguise. I've been known to be perfectionistic in my attempt to not be a perfectionist.

Perfectionism isn't...

"[Perfectionism] is not possessiveness, orderliness, rigidity, conscientiousness, or achievement motivation. Although some of these features can at times coexist with perfectionism, they do not constitute perfectionism."[3]

Perfectionism is not having high standards or a value for accuracy. It's not self-motivating or wanting to do your best. It's not having drive and determination. It's not merely hard work. It's not striving for excellence or a healthy appetite for learning.

Perfectionism is not the same as **self-improvement**. Perfectionism tells us there is something inherently wrong about us and, if only we could fix those flaws, we would be worthy of love and approval. Often, perfectionism is rooted in praise for our achievements and performance in our early years; perfectionists are still chasing the A grade, the gold star, and the nod of approval from the people we look up to. We start to believe that our identity is synonymous with our accomplishments and with pleasing others: *"I am what I achieve and how well I perform and please."*

It's definitely not **resilient**. It's not adaptable, flexible or responsive. It does not have grace under fire.

Perfectionism is not the **key to success** we so often tell ourselves it is. Research shows perfectionism hampers achievement and is correlated with depression, anxiety, addiction and life paralysis, or missed opportunities.[4] Perfectionism undermines

---

[3] ibid.

[4] Thomas Curran and Andrew P. Hill (2019) Perfectionism Is Increasing Over Time: A Meta-Analysis of Birth Cohort Differences From 1989 to 2016. *American Psychological Association Psychological Bulletin*. Vol. 145, No. 4, 410 – 429. Morgan-Lowes KL, Clarke PJF, Hoiles KJ, Shu CY, Watson HJ, Dunlop PD, Egan SJ (2019) The relationships between perfectionism, anxiety and depression across time in paediatric eating disorders. *Eat Behav*. 2019 Aug;34. Kawamura, K.Y., Hunt, S.L., Frost, R.O. *et al* (2001)Perfectionism, Anxiety, and Depression: Are the Relationships Independent?. *Cognitive Therapy and Research*. 25, 291–301

us; we make ourselves small in the face of the fear of failing, making mistakes, not meeting people's expectations, and being criticised.

It is absolutely not the same as a heart-led, soul-fuelled desire to do something amazing.

Perfectionism is not **a choice**. It's not undone by sheer willpower alone. It cannot be fought, battled or worked on. If being hard on yourself worked, it would have worked already.

Perfectionism isn't Healthy but it is Normal

There is no such thing as 'healthy' perfectionism, in my experience. How can something so painful ever be healthy?

Perfectionism is a completely normal human response. It's a survival strategy, one that has worked really well for a lot of us otherwise we would have never bothered with it in the first place!

I know lots of perfectionists, myself included, cling to our perfectionist strategies like drowning rats on a piece of wood in the unpredictable waters of life. Because letting go of that survival strategy without anything else to support us is naturally terrifying. I've often found myself asking questions like "how will I ever get anything done if I'm not pushing myself?" and "what's the point of me if I'm not getting things done?".

Funnily enough, this is that perfectionistic all-or-nothing thinking revealing itself. You don't have to choose between life-withering perfectionism and being a complete slacker. There IS a happy medium, a place that can hold both the parts of us that are ambitious and driven AND the parts that long for ease and flow.

An Antidote to Perfectionism

"Stop trying to 'fix' yourself; you're NOT broken! You are perfectly imperfect and powerful beyond measure."
~ Steve Maraboli

Perfectionism is a survival strategy. It keeps us feeling safe, even at the expense of meaningful connections with others and ultimately ourselves. It's an unconscious lens through which we interact with the world.

Somewhere along the line, we learned that it wasn't okay to be us. That we need to control, even manipulate, and present the right version of ourselves. That we needed to manage how others experienced us so they wouldn't see past the veneer.

Perfectionism is a shield that prevents us from being seen.

Perfectionism leaves no space for raw, unfiltered, authenticity. It assumes that the act of simply being human can be studied, improved, and perfected. And it determines the measure of one's goodness and value by how thoroughly and tirelessly you seek to be better.

It is an exhausting and perpetually disappointing way to live: the work is never good enough and the job is never done. There is always room for improvement.

Perfectionism is born in fear. Fear of being yourself. Fear of not being enough. Fear of being too much.

> *"Fear of making a mistake. Fear of disappointing others. Fear of failure. Fear of success."*
> *~ Michael Law.*

Perfectionism is dressed up as a deep commitment to drive and ambition. It masquerades as being conscientious, thorough and careful.

For a long time, I clung to perfectionism like a woman drowning in a sea of my own self-doubt.

It's been how I create my identity, worth, and right to be in this world. It's driven me to achieve and strive for success – or so I thought. As I've come back home to my body, I've come to realise that perfectionism is actually "self-abuse of the highest order", in the words of Anne Wilson Schaef.

It's toxic.

The paradox of perfectionism is that its pursuit does not lead to a fuller, richer, and more rewarding existence, because nothing will ever be good enough – including you. It simply eats away at your innate wisdom and truth, creates emptiness, and reduces you to a project without an end.

Perfectionism is a trap. It gets in the way of us deeply knowing ourselves, our needs, our desires, and our intuition. It's a barrier to connecting fully with another human being. It keeps us from the most basic things we desire as human beings – meaning, aliveness, and connection.

> *"Perfectionism is a dream killer, because it's just fear disguised as trying to do your best."*
> *~ Mastin Kipp*

Perfectionism eroded my trust in myself. A perfectionist cannot be in relationship with their own body and their own experience because that body, that experience, is inherently imperfect. And so we harden, we constrict, we move into our heads to prepare and plan for every possible contingency and consequence in a desperate and never-ending search for the right answer.

The antidote to perfectionism is wholeness.

| **Wholeness** – *noun*:

- the condition of being sound in body;
- the quality or state of being without restriction, exception, or qualification;
- the state of forming a complete and harmonious whole; unity;
- the state of being unbroken or undamaged.

Wholeness is to be authentic. Wholeness is understanding my body's needs, desires and wisdom. Wholeness is feeling and responding to my rhythms. It's feeling my feelings and not being overwhelmed by them.

Wholeness is an invitation to come home to ourselves.

When we allow ourselves to receive all the sensory and emotional information in our bodies, we create the space to make conscious choices about what we do next. Rather than reacting habitually from perfectionism, we can choose our response. Nothing is ever to fix, shift or change – simply notice. We stop resisting the flow of life within us and we can be present with what is.

To my deep relief and complete surprise, wholeness still allows me to get things done in the world. I feared that, without my perfectionism driving me, I would end up small, weak, or unable to take action. My experience has been quite the opposite. Without the constant self-bullying, my mind is becoming more creative. Without the tension and tightness in my body, I feel free – I feel more in all senses of that word.

Wholeness opens more possibilities for succeeding because I stopped fighting myself along the way.

Wholeness is a radical act.

Wholeness means understanding that you are enough. That your unique collection of traits, gifts and wounds is all that is required to qualify as enough (and it is unique – in roughly 50,000 years of human existence, there have been over 108 billion people born and not one of them has lived your life.[5])

| **Flawsome** – *adjective*:

an individual who embraces their "flaws" and knows they are awesome regardless.

That's what wholeness means to me. It's the ability to embrace every aspect of who we are – quirks, flaws, dirty little secrets, shadows as well as our brilliance, talents and gifts – be-

---

[5] https://scorecard.prb.org/howmanypeoplehaveeverlivedonearth/

cause it is that whole package that makes us unique and awesome.

Learning to be true to ourselves, to dance to our own beat, is liberating.

After millennia of falling for the myth of perfectionism, we need to remember a different way of being.

We can choose to let ourselves be seen.

We can allow ourselves the possibility that other people love us for exactly who we truly are. That people want to get to know the real us, not the masks we wear. That our genuine, authentic, raw presence is a gift that other people don't merely tolerate, but deeply desire in their lives.

It takes courage, strength, and commitment – luckily, skills recovering perfectionists have in spades. The medicine is channelling those capacities away from hiding and controlling, towards allowing and being open.

It starts with radical self-compassion and welcoming everything. Even the parts we want to change, even the parts we think are deeply unlovable. Welcome it all.

The practice of welcoming everything is one of equanimity. It's the power of simply turning towards what is, with awareness and curiosity. It's an invitation to become conscious.

When we allow ourselves to receive all the sensory and emotional information in our bodies, we stop resisting the flow of life within us and we can be present with what is.

"What self-acceptance does is open up more possibilities of succeeding because you aren't fighting yourself along the way."
~ Shannon Ables

We say yes to ourselves; we give ourselves permission to feel everything our body is telling us in this moment. We trust.

This is a gentle revolution in a world that profits from our self-doubt.

When we start by simply noticing, we realise that nothing needs to be fixed, shifted or changed. You are not broken. You are a human being having a human experience.

By saying yes to our full experience, we create the space to make conscious choices about what we do next. Rather than reacting, we choose our response. We decide to act differently because we want to, not because we're lacking.

In this book, I'm not seeking to change anything about you. **You're already enough as you are.** You don't have to change yourself to change your life. Self-improvement is not required here. Unlearning perfectionism is one of the few paths of growth that welcomes un-improving and letting your standards "slip".

Instead, I will present you with a new paradigm to redesign your relationship with yourself, including your perfectionist tendencies. My wish for you is to know that you are wholly flawsome.

First, how do you even spot the signs and symptoms of perfectionism?

Five Flavours of Perfectionism

"Perfectionism sucks the air out of your uniqueness and leaves you empty, away from who you could become."
~ *Darryl Stewart Wellness*

The more I've been paying attention to perfectionism, the more I've realised that the stereotype of a perfectionist is a gross oversimplification of a complex pattern of behaviour.

That stereotype allowed me to deny I was a perfectionist for many years. I didn't consciously strive for perfection and I definitely didn't consider myself perfect. Quite the opposite – I never felt good enough to be a perfectionist.

Perfectionism shows up in different ways for different people at different points in their lives. I've noticed five flavours of perfectionism that, together, create a more nuanced picture of perfectionism.

Before I introduce you to these five characters, I want to say something about labels.

Labels can be funny things.

I've found understanding more about perfectionism, including these five particular manifestations of it, has helped me see my patterns more clearly. I think these kinds of labels also help to normalise very human experiences that I can easily think are just me being broken in a world where everyone else has it sorted. Knowing there is a label for these behaviours helps me understand that it's not just me.

Labels, however, are completely unhelpful when they put us in a box and become fixed in our identity. They can turn normal human behaviours and experiences into pathologies. It's why I'm getting more sensitive about saying "I'm a perfectionist" because I'm not. I'm doing perfectionism. I'm a human being who happens to be Vix-ing in a perfectionist way some of the time (alright, quite a bit of the time!).

I offer these five flavours of perfectionism in the spirit of the former. I hope these help you understand yourself better and bring a deeper level of awareness and acceptance. They might even let you find a little bit of humour and allow you to laugh at yourself – I find us recovering perfectionists can be a little uptight!

Let me introduce you to **The Fastidious Five**.

The Always On Over-Doer

The Over-doer sets extremely high – often unrealistic or unattainable - standards and goals, usually without even being able to clearly articulate what those goals are. You're often impatient, expecting to achieve your goals quickly and getting upset when things stall. The goalposts are constantly moving. When you do reach your goals, you often move on to the next project before celebrating your achievements, often dismissing them as not important or noteworthy.

You tend to not appreciate what you do well, instead focusing on what went wrong or what you should have done differently. You might even believe that there is no excuse for mistakes and so self-compassion and 'letting yourself off the hook' are weaknesses. Even positive feedback can be scary because deep down, you believe you could always be better. This can make it difficult for you to appreciate life because you're always thinking about what you need to change and this can lead you to feel a little bit dissatisfied without really understanding why.

It's hard for you to enjoy the journey because you're so focused on the end result. You have an insatiable drive to make things the best they can be and you believe in the immutable value of hard work. Working hard is a good thing in your world. This makes it easy for you to spend way more time on something than the task actually merits.

You hate not being good at things or making mistakes, which can be tricky when you're always pushing yourself to learn more. You believe being good at something means you no longer make mistakes. At the same time, you hate things being easy so you tend to overcomplicate things so they feel worthwhile and interesting. You're more likely to quit than to continue to do something imperfectly.

You might even reject the idea of being an overachiever — surely that is reserved for the Forbes 30 Under 30 list or other people who have accomplished so much. But you can't shake the nagging feeling that you're never doing enough; there's always something else you could be doing.

The Perpetual Procrastinator

The Perpetual Procrastinator wants conditions to be exactly right before starting a task. You can be bothered by a sensation that everything needs to be 'just right'; there is always a reason why it would be better to do it later. Deep down, you're scared you might do it wrong or fail completely. You always want more time to get things exactly right, but you often misjudge the time it takes to get projects done, leaving you feeling flustered and short of time. It can also be hard for you to finish a task as it's never quite good enough.

You avoid, consciously or not, activities or tasks where you won't be the best or perfect with your first attempt. You often give up easily when things get hard and move on to something that you think will be easier to achieve or distract yourself with something that isn't in service of your long-term goals (hello, social media scroll hole!). You're likely to say to yourself "I'll be happy when..." so find yourself living for the future, rather than focusing on the present.

You can be full of amazing ideas and yet find getting started on something new is scary and you'll always find an excuse to not put yourself out there. This can lead you to give up on projects and your dreams either because you don't believe in yourself or you're scared of what might happen if it goes well.

The Over-Caring People Pleaser

The People Pleaser strives for and thrives on external validation. You love to be praised and recognised by other people. Your sense of self and worthiness comes from outside yourself, from other people's judgement of you. This makes receiving criticism a shame-inducing experience and you can feel anxious about being judged.

You always worry about what other people think of you, even though you intellectually know that it's not healthy. You tend to compare yourself to others, usually negatively; you put other people on a pedestal. It's much easier for you to judge your self-worth based on what you *assume* people think of you. You prefer to 'fit in' and make sure other people are having a good time, rather than being truly authentic and belonging in your own right. You might be so used to doing this that you've lost touch with who you really are.

You tend to defer to other people's wants and needs; you might even be proud of this. The reality may be that you don't even know what you want because you're so used to being vigilant toward other people.

You find yourself going over conversations after-the-fact, picking apart everything that you might have done wrong. Even if someone said they had a good time with you, you worry that you somehow upset them and you can easily blame yourself for other people's bad moods or uncomfortable emotions.

The Paralysed Over-Thinker

There are no shades of grey in the world of the Over-Thinker. It's all or nothing, always or never. In considering a challenge or a problem, you tend to see two binary choices; it's either this or that, with nothing in between. You tend to think in absolute rather than nuanced language. You evaluate your work by what it is not, rather than what it is. You are overly critical of yourself and talk to yourself harshly, in a way that you would never speak to anyone else. That inner critic can run rampant!

You tend to stress over decisions, either not making a decision at all or second-guessing yourself and changing your mind after you make a choice. You find it hard to trust yourself when making big decisions. You love researching topics before you make a decision. This can start as fun but can quickly lead you into paralysis when you become overwhelmed by the amount of information and the number of options available.

You might have excelled academically at school and have been rewarded for your intellect. You're likely to spend a lot of time in your head, with your thoughts going round and round, and you might find it difficult to be present in your body. In fact, you're often judgemental and self-conscious about your physical body and it can be hard for you to let go and relax your body.

The Holding-On-Too-Tight Control Freak

The Control Freak loves to live in the future to ward off potential problems. You tend to micromanage, always thinking hours, days, weeks, or even months ahead of yourself. You always like to know exactly what's going to happen. You can't stand chaos and uncertainty; perversely, you might choose a lifestyle that forces change on you as you can get a buzz from reestablishing order. You're happiest with a plan and a spreadsheet, maybe a checklist too. When things go wrong, you need to find someone or something to blame – usually yourself or your nearest and dearest.

Uncomfortable emotions can be scary because they make you feel out of control. And yet, you often experience disproportionate emotional turmoil to imperfect details or things not working out as you wanted. You are bothered by a sensation that everything needs to be 'just right'. If something is not perfect, it's not worth it. Good enough is not in your vocabulary; the very concept sparks an almost allergic reaction.

You try to manage and control other people – all in the name of progress and improvement – so they don't disrupt your carefully laid plans. This makes it difficult to delegate or trust others as, deep down, you don't believe they'll do as good a job as you can.

A Pause to Reflect

What flavour are you?

Most people I've met who have perfectionist tendencies have a mix of flavours, like a very odd ice-cream sundae. Personally, I most identify with the over-doer and the control freak with a little dash of people-pleasing. Having read the descriptions above, which ones had you shouting "that's me!"?

How You Do One Thing Is How You Do Everything

"Understanding of life begins with the understanding of patterns."
~ Fritjof Capra

Our bodies are more than tools to help us do stuff in our lives, directed by our heads.

Our posture, movement and body language – our shaping – determine how we experience the present moment and the choices we have available to us to shape our future. The way we hold our bodies, move around and interact in the world is also habitual. It becomes a way of managing and expressing who we are; our self-identity is inseparable from our embodiment.

One metaphor for this is the hologram.

Just as each piece of a hologram contains the entire virtual image, so a pattern in one aspect of our lives tends to be the pattern we have in all aspects of our lives. In the same way, each of our cells contains our complete genetic code; the code in one cell is the same as the code in all cells and, together, they form a larger whole.

When we can start to see these patterns, we can start to

practise something different. We create the opportunity for more choice.

This is the essence of embodiment and it's a fundamental part of how I coach clients, and how each of us can create transformation in our lives.

Let me tell you about how running revealed one of my holograms.

I love running. I love the satisfaction, the endorphin high, and the peace as I run through the rice fields near my home in Bali. I've been running for years, even completing a marathon in Uganda.

There's one major difference with my running these days. I'm working with an auto-immune thyroid condition at the moment and it's really important I don't overly stress my body. That means keeping my heart rate down.

The idea of running slower than I'm capable of was so incredibly frustrating. Do less than I could? Are you high?!

In true Vix-fashion, on my first heart-rate zone run, I realised that slower meant I had way more energy at the halfway point. So I ran further and found I could be satisfied with slower as long as it meant more by other measures.

This experience led to two realisations about how this reflects my approach to life. It revealed my embodied patterns, my hologram.

The first realisation was understanding somatically that **slowing down could be helpful**. Slowing down allowed me to go further and do more. My stamina improved. I could enjoy the view more. I could slow down and still feel good.

That feels important to me as an occasionally stressed-out overachiever. Slowing down can mean more, not less.

Who knew?

The second realisation was much less palatable.

I'm still operating this story that more means better.

That stuff about the view and feeling good were afterthoughts. I really struggled with the idea of my run not being as hard, and therefore as worthwhile, as it had been when I could run to my maximum every time.

As I'm writing this, I notice I feel shame admitting this to you. I'm judging myself for still having this old operating code buried in my psyche. Why haven't I fixed myself yet so I am a perfect, unflawed human being?

Naming these feelings helps me welcome the part of myself that judges and criticises. It helps me welcome the part that does believe more means better. And it helps me come back to my Self, where I can have compassion for the patterns I'm seeing play out in me.

I'm reminded that these deeply-held beliefs never really go away. The neural pathways in my brain that equate more with better will always be there.

But that doesn't mean I have to let them rule me. I can learn that sometimes more isn't better, just as I'm learning that slowing down is not the death sentence to my productivity I once thought it was. And so can you.

You can choose to listen to your body rather than the story that more equals better or less means weak. Those stories might still play, like radio stations in your mind; you don't have to pay attention to them.

A Pause to Reflect

Take a moment to reflect on your embodied patterns. What are your holograms around perfectionism and productivity?

Ask yourself where this would be useful in your life. Where can you notice the stories without blindly assuming they're 'true'? Where can you listen more deeply to how your body feels to guide you? How could you practice something different so you have more choice?

In the next chapters, I'll share two more holograms that I think are common amongst perfectionists.

Perfectionism Is a Lonely Game

"Alone we can do so little; together we can do so much."
~ Helen Keller

For as long as I remember, I've thought of myself as a lone wolf. I can be fiercely independent with a deeply held belief that I have to do things on my own.

Some of this is part of who I am. There are (embarrassing) family videos of me as a three-year-old proudly declaring "look, Daddy, I did it all by myself!"

I've also come to realise that the roots of this story are a survival strategy. In a world of regular moving and boarding school, 'needing' other people felt dangerous and unreliable. I imagine that I doubled down on that natural independence to shut myself away from the world so other people couldn't disappoint me, hurt me, or let me down.

Being a lone wolf suited me. As an RAF Intelligence Officer, I often had to spend hours researching and reading before presenting my analysis. My work had an inherently solitary aspect to it which suited me down to the ground.

And yet, I was deeply lonely for much of my twenties and early thirties.

As proficient as I had become at squashing down my feelings, loneliness gnawed at my insides. I saw people around me forming long-term friendships and relationships as I stood quietly on the sidelines, having taken myself out of the game almost entirely.

As a full-blown perfectionist back then, I automatically assumed there was something wrong with me. Maybe I had missed the lessons where everyone seemed to learn how to make friends.

I remember this version of myself with tenderness and compassion. I was doing my best to navigate life with the skills, stories and strategies I had learned that would keep me safe. And they were pretty effective in so much that I had a lot of what I wanted in life. Yet, I knew deep down that they were coming at a cost.

The irony that all my work now is based around being in connection with people is not lost on me. But it's more than just the focus of my work. I've come to realise how critical friendship and community are to my vitality.

It's fun to work with people, to collaborate and create something with others. My work is better for exposing it to different views and perspectives. I feel so full after spending time with people who I feel comfortable being wholly myself with. Not to mention that physical touch, especially cuddles, helps us regulate our nervous systems:

"We need four hugs a day for survival. We need eight hugs a day for maintenance. We need 12 hugs a day for growth."
~ Virginia Satir [6]

---

[6] https://draxe.com/health/hugs/

I'm learning that my stories of not being able to rely on other people, of not needing them, and of it being somehow inherently more worthwhile if I do everything myself are no longer true. I can choose something different.

I don't think this story is unique to me. I think being a lone wolf is a trait of perfectionism. It's part of that defensive shield that prevents us from being seen. It helps us keep people at arm's length so they can't see past the perfect veneer. It stops us from asking for help and comfort. It prevents us from getting our basic needs met (including the twelve cuddles we need a day to thrive).

Stages of Development

Independence is a stage of development. These stages might correlate with certain stages of our life, and as we move through them, we integrate that stage of wisdom into our being so that we can access each stage as we need to.

We all start life being dependent. We rely on others to meet our needs when we haven't yet individuated. As we grow, we learn independence and start to venture into the world on our own. We understand ourselves as separate from others and develop our own opinions and values. We can act for ourselves.

As a perfectionist, I think my development stopped here at this second stage for many years. The only options I had were doing it all by myself or waiting helplessly for someone to rescue me.

There is a third stage.

Independence can never be complete. We are always reliant on something beyond us; chances are you didn't grow all the food you ate today or make your own clothes or generate your own electricity. Independence is by degree and understanding that is to step into *interdependence*. To be interdependent is to recognise the limits of being an individual. It's both, and: to embrace all your strengths and capabilities *and* to embrace your need for something beyond yourself. It's the ability to ask for help because the whole is greater than the sum of its parts.

I saw this dance so clearly when I got married. I didn't want to be dependent on my partner and I could see that my habit of independence would undermine my desire for the type of partnership I wanted for us.

And it is a dance. Sometimes, you're following; sometimes, you're leading. Together, you create something beautiful.

A Pause to Reflect

I invite you to be curious about your stories around (hyper) independence. What stories and beliefs do you have about asking for help and needing others? How have those stories served you? What cost might they have? How would you like to rewrite them?

Being Busy Keeps Us Safe

"I go too fast to see much, only the tops of everything. I've got to prowl slow some time through this country."
~ Will Rogers

Being busy, being productive, achieving and overdoing have been my norm for most of my life. If I'm really honest, this is still my default mode.

I need to do or be more to be complete. It's never enough. There is always more I could be doing in each and every domain of my life. Not only in work, but how I show up for other people, my activism, how much I exercise...whatever it is, *do more*.

I can ignore my own needs and stress arousal limits to the point of becoming overwhelmed and exhausted and yet still keep dragging myself forward. When I'm busy, I don't feel hungry. I can push through and make sure the job gets done.

That was really useful during my military training when a Corporal was screaming at me to leopard-crawl faster. It was still useful when I was working 16-hour days every day for 6 months on operational deployments in the Middle East.

It was the perfect strategy to deny, suppress and mask pain, ignore my physiological needs and override my own limits. Striving was a way to avoid feeling.

Busyness is the avoidance of connection.

When I'm busy, I can avoid being with myself and all those big, messy feelings. I can avoid being in connection with others; I can avoid the risk of vulnerability and intimacy.

Being busy feels safe to me.

There's something that feels inherently threatening in slowing down and relaxing. Something in my system equates softness with weakness. I exacerbate this relationship by going until exhaustion forces me to collapse, leaving me small and defenceless.

At some point in my life, I learned to prove my worth and earn love and attention through doing, not being. Whilst I intellectually understand that's not true, I still have an embodied pattern that continues to rely on these outdated behaviours, no matter how outdated they are.

You might be thinking that striving is essential for growth. That it's necessary to force yourself outside your comfort zone or that the only way to build resilience is to work through challenges. I disagree. Sustainable growth doesn't come from constantly pushing and forcing. Our soul deeply desires growth; it can't help but naturally expand. The only way this expansion is sustainable is when our nervous system is rooted in safety. We can only build resilience when we give ourselves time to recover and integrate. Will it still be uncomfortable? Absolutely, and the most effective way to grow over time is by alternating periods of discomfort with periods of gentleness, re-regulation and integration.

Yet all too often, I'm onto the next thing before the paint has dried.

When I slow down, I give myself the gift of awareness. I can recognise my own needs and respect my limits. Slowing down stops me from swinging between the highs of overdoing and stress and the lows of shame and not-enoughness. I can see that my needs and limits change in accordance with my rhythms and cycles.

Allowing myself to *be* turns out to be less scary than I thought. On the contrary, it's richer and deeper. Life can be full, rather than busy, when I take the time to be present. It's how I live up to my desire to have a life I don't need a holiday from.

Slowing down isn't for perfection or even optimisation. It's for wholeness.

A Pause to Reflect

How do you use busyness as a strategy to keep you safe? What stories do you have about slowing down or even stopping for a while?

This Road Leads to Burnout

"Burnout is what happens when you try to avoid being human for too long."
~ Michael Gungor

Overwhelm and burnout are the natural consequences of unchecked perfectionism. We often habituate to these ways of being and sacrifice our health, our relationships and our souls on the altar of achievement, especially in a world where burnout is becoming more and more common.[7]

We're terrified to slow down because we're scared we'll never get going again. The irony is if we don't slow down in a deliberate, mindful way, our bodies slam on the brakes at some point — usually the most inconvenient point possible — and we crash head first into burnout, which can take months to come back from.

---

[7] Searches in Google give us a glimpse of the growing focus on burnout. In 2015, 210 people searched for "occupational burnout" globally. By 2020, that figure had risen to 5,400 — a rise of 184% compared to the year before. It's a similar story with searches for "burnout symptoms", with 27,100 searching the term in 2020, compared to 4,400 in 2015. https://www.microbizmag.co.uk/burnout-statistics-uk/

What is burnout?

Burnout is a state of chronic stress and physical, mental and emotional exhaustion that impedes your ability to function effectively.

It's insidious. It's like a slow puncture, gradually deflating our very lifeforce over time. It makes it hard to recognise, especially for those of us who are already pretty disconnected from our bodies and their signals.

Burnout isn't the same as stress

One way to think about stress is as too much. It's believing that there are too many demands, too much pressure, too much to cope with physically or mentally. Too much to do, too many responsibilities, too many expectations, and it's all too much to handle.

Being burnt out is like feeling there isn't enough. No matter how hard you work or try to concentrate, you aren't getting enough done. You haven't got enough strength emotionally or physically to take on a new task or face the new day. It feels like you've got nothing left to give, like you aren't good enough, and you may struggle to see the point in even trying.

It's moving from a state of continual hyperarousal and living life with the accelerator fully down to a state of hypoarousal and the brakes being stuck on.

Who's at risk?

Perfectionists and overachievers can be particularly vulnerable to burnout. With our 'can-do' personalities and self-sufficient identities driven by high standards, we can easily miss the warning signs as we can get stuck in our heads. Tending to push through and dismiss long hours, taking on heavier workloads, and putting more pressure on ourselves to excel, we can risk pushing through our body's physical signs that they are overworking until they have got no more to give.

Burnout doesn't have to be only work-related. I've seen first-time mums burnout from chronic people-pleasing and over-giving.

Having burnt out once and nearly burned myself out a second time just a year later, I've realised that I can never stop paying attention to the signs. As a recovering perfectionist, I will probably always have a tendency to inadvertently push myself to the edge and beyond.

Signs to watch out for

You're constantly tired, even after getting a full night's sleep.

Feeling tired all the time is a clear sign that your body is suffering from chronic stress. Our stress response system isn't designed to be activated all the time and, unfortunately, modern life is full of things our minds and bodies perceive as threats. When we keep pushing ourselves to be 'on' all the time, we get hooked on using adrenaline, cortisol, caffeine and sugar to keep us going. We've convinced ourselves – and we've been convinced by the cultures we work in – that this is how we need to work to get it all done.

The problem is that more, bigger, and faster generates value that is narrow, shallow, and short-term.

One consequence of relying on our stress hormones as a source of energy, for example, is that the prefrontal cortex begins to shut down in response to the oversaturation of stress hormones. We become more reactive and less capable of thinking clearly, reflectively or creatively.

You keep putting off the same tasks for days at a time.

Procrastination is another clear symptom that you're losing the impetus and resolve to keep pace with your current workload. The sense of apathy, and oftentimes anxiety or hopelessness, that you feel from burnout can result in overlooked and incomplete work. You just don't seem to have the drive to tackle the to-do list and instead find the time spinning away from you.

You might struggle to concentrate or pay attention or have a harder time than normal making decisions, especially about small, inconsequential things.

Whilst the procrastination gremlin strikes everyone at one point or another, it's a clear sign you're on the road to burnout when it's a constant companion over weeks.

You keep getting ill or putting on weight.

Stress and the immune system were first linked by a ten-year study that took place in the 1980s and 1990s.[8] In the study, researchers discovered that medical students experienced a decline in immunity during the three-day period in which they took exams. The extended period of stress caused by the tests

---

[8] https://www.apa.org/topics/stress/body

caused their bodies to stop producing the cells needed to fight off infection.

You might find yourself suffering from the cold or flu, even in the middle of summer. You could feel sore and achy on a regular or even constant basis. Some who suffer from burnout even get diagnosed with chronic conditions as a result of their stress.

Illness isn't the only way that burnout and excessive stress can have a negative impact on your physical health. Excess cortisol sends a signal to your body that you're in danger and need to hold on to your calories in the form of body fat, in case of an emergency. So even if you're eating well and exercising, you start to gain weight. And excess cortisol, especially if combined with a lack of sleep, causes the body to crave foods that are high in sugar or fat, making it that much harder to stick to a healthy diet.

You rely on unhealthy coping mechanisms.

In an effort to make ourselves feel better, it's easy to resort to strategies that provide short-term relief but that numb out, avoid or even exacerbate the underlying issue. Obvious unhealthy coping mechanisms include self-medicating with the likes of caffeine, alcohol, drugs, food, sex, TV, smoking, or social media. You probably don't even think of it as self-medicating; there's a cultural norm of having an alcoholic drink to wind down after work or needing a cup of coffee (or three) to get started in the morning. What would happen if you didn't have a glass of wine or spend the evening binge-watching TV? How would you feel? How often do you need these strategies? Once in a while is human; every day or a feeling of not being able to cope without them might be a sign you're numbing out.

Withdrawing from friends and family is a common response amongst perfectionists, who tend to believe they're self-sufficient and struggle to ask for help. Isolating yourself makes it harder for you to regulate your nervous system and keeps you stuck in the loop of needing to do it all, all by yourself.

Alternatively, you might be relying on apparently healthy tools – yoga, meditation, centring – that give you just enough capacity to keep going. They keep you stuck on the road to burnout because you're dealing with the symptoms in the moment without addressing the underlying causes. If you have a sense of needing a practice to survive or stay sane, that could be a sign that a healthy activity has become a less healthy coping mechanism.

You're always 'on', even when you're taking some downtime.

So many of us have internalised the feeling that we should be working all the time. We find ourselves feeling guilty for taking a break or time off. We start to view rest as a sign of weakness and of not wanting to achieve our goals enough.

Perhaps you've thought about taking a break at some point and found yourself thinking "do I really deserve one?" and/or "I could be working on something else right now."

We're so used to engaging in telic activities – those with a goal or purpose, a project that can be finished or completed – we view rest in the same vein. But rest is inherently an atelic activity, one we engage in for the sake of it – like going for a walk for the pleasure of walking rather than to get your step count up.

So even when you do take a break, your perfectionism still kicks in with the expectation that the downtime will be meaningful, even productive. Rest is something to be done in order to achieve something else.

Even when I am relaxing, I notice that I'm still striving to do it "right" or to make sure that it's worthwhile.

You don't have to be 100mph all the time.

Having limitations doesn't make you a failure and doesn't mean you're not enough. It means you're human and you have finite energy. Our energy is finite and as soon as you think it isn't, burnout becomes a problem.

If being a busy person is part of our identity, it can be really hard to accept that we need to slow down. It's so easy to see relaxation as a waste of time, taking us away from something more productive. And of course, we need to be productive to be successful, right?

What I've learned from my own experience of burnout and from managing stress in conflict zones is that downtime is always worthwhile. As human beings, we simply cease to operate if we don't create the conditions to relax.

As capable as our nervous systems are to respond to threats and stress, they are also designed to rest and recuperate after stress. In the so-called "Rest and Digest" mode, our bodies naturally heal and recover. As our bodies soften and relax, so do our minds, clearing themselves of old ideas and making space for new ones.

We need to learn the art of stillness and creating opportunities to turn our attention inwards and to tend to whatever's there. And that's where we're heading next.

(Many of these symptoms are associated with other illnesses and conditions so if you identify with this list, please see a health professional to rule out any other underlying causes).

A Way to Radical Self-Acceptance

"No amount of self-improvement can make up for any lack of self-acceptance."
~ Robert Holden

My inner perfectionist has this idea that I need to be better, to fix myself, to be constantly growing and improving.

But what if I didn't need to fix myself? What if what I need isn't another hack, another expert, or another five-step plan?

What if I don't need to be fixed? What if I am completely whole, with all my flaws, imperfections, strengths and beauty? Maybe it's not my perceived imperfections and shortcomings holding me back but the idea that I need to be and that I need to be fixed. What if I could let go of the notion that if I fix this or that, I would be happy? What if I could find peace with exactly how I am?

As I write that, I notice a part of me seize up in fear. I tighten the muscles around my chest, belly and throat. "But how will I get anything done if I'm at peace?" a voice cries out. "Surely, I have to keep improving in order to be loved?".

Oh, my love. I hear that's how you feel. I hear your fear and your longing to be loved. And those are just stories.

You came into this world whole. A soft little body housing pure light. As you've grown, so has your body. Your mind developed. You learnt things about this world and you learned to respond to it in a way that would keep you safe and belonging.

Gabor Mate describes two fundamental needs we have as children: secure attachment and authentic expression. We will always choose our sense of belonging and will subconsciously suppress our authenticity for the sake of our safety and survival. So you developed ways to suppress your authenticity to keep yourself safe. Of course you did; your body is intelligent and adaptive. You built armour and developed patterns of behaviour to keep yourself feeling safe. And you hid your light away.

That pure light, that wholeness, that total worthiness is still in you.

The work then isn't to change or improve or better yourself. It's to come home to yourself. To drop the armour. To take the walls down.

It's a returning.

A remembering.

I invite you to start by stopping.

One thing I notice perfectionists have in common is that we immediately want to get into action, to fix the problem. That makes complete sense and it's reinforcing the underlying belief that this is a problem that needs to be fixed.

Instead, before doing anything, what would it feel like to notice what's happening? To pay attention and be curious first before deciding if anything needs to change?

The practice of welcoming everything is one of equanimity. It's the power to remain undisturbed by the experience of emotions, pain, and life. It's not indifference. It's not condoning. It's the power of simply turning towards what is with awareness and curiosity.

Welcoming everything is an invitation to become more fully conscious.

When we allow ourselves to receive all the sensory and emotional information in our bodies, we create the space to make conscious choices about what we do next. Rather than reacting, we can choose our response. Nothing is ever to fix, shift or change – simply notice. We stop resisting the flow of life within us and we can be present with what is.

"What self-acceptance does is open up more possibilities of succeeding because you aren't fighting yourself along the way."
~ Shannon Ables

We say yes to ourselves; we give ourselves permission to feel everything our body is telling us.

From here, from this place of saying yes to our full experience, we can decide that we want to be able to do something more because we want to, not because we're lacking.

Change without acceptance is sacrificing our authenticity for safety. Welcoming everything is the key to holding the polarities of loving myself as I am and embracing my desire to learn new ways of being. When I notice that my experience – my world – is a complete and whole human experience – for good and ill – then I'm giving myself the gift of learning because I'm excited, not because I'm scared. I'm full-filled, not lacking.

"The World is perfect as it is, including my desire to change it."
~ Ram Dass

A Pause to Reflect

What are the experiences or aspects of yourself that feel difficult to welcome? What would it be like to notice that difficulty with more compassion and curiosity?

The Dance Between Self-Acceptance, Self-Improvement and Never Being Good Enough

"We don't have to wait until we are on our deathbed to realize what a waste of our precious lives it is to carry the belief that something is wrong with us."
~ Tara Brach

In 2020, I spent nearly a year studying to be an embodied coach and facilitator. A core element of this journey was committing to an embodied practice for 6 months to enhance an area where we were underdeveloped, and thereby develop more range.

In true overachiever style, I wanted to do ALL the practises. I saw all the places I could be "better", all the areas I wasn't perfect. I wanted to push myself in my desire to be a world-class facilitator.

I felt stuck. I felt overwhelmed. I felt small and inadequate.

The breakthrough came for me when I realised that nothing I did was ever going to be enough if I couldn't learn how to accept myself as whole *as I am right now*.

Not when I was less serious. Not when I had more clients. Not when I was "better". But exactly as I am.

What if I never did another training course? What if I never went to another workshop? Could I still live with myself?

I realised that this was my opportunity to lean into my edge and learn to do nothing. If I could find a way to love myself regardless, then any other practice I chose to do would be just that – a choice, rather than another way to sell myself on the story that I'm not enough.

Something about this still feels radical to me as a self-confessed personal development junkie. I've often found myself wrestling with the question of how my desire to better myself sits with my desire for self-acceptance.

I'm not the only one; a client asked me:

"At what point do we accept this is who we are and work with that? Or is change always possible?"

My take is that change is always possible. In fact, it's inevitable.

But change that isn't grounded in self-acceptance is never fulfilling. If I'm approaching my growth from a place of scarcity and not-enoughness, there will always be another upgrade.

This form of self-improvement is a black hole for your energy, time and money. Because it never fills the hole that self-rejection creates. You can't feel you belong in the world if you don't feel you belong in your own being.

Perfectionism tells us there is always something more to do. It convinces us that happiness and wholeness are just over the crest of the next mountain we need to climb. It masquerades as a healthy drive for learning when, in fact, it's a product of our sense of not-enoughness.

And so my answer to the question "do we accept ourselves or do we keep seeking to improve" is "both, and".

I can hold the polarity of deep self-acceptance and still desire change.

Paradoxically, this might be one of the hardest things I find about recovering from perfectionism. Surrender, softening, accepting... Even writing those words, I'm aware of the parts of me that judge that as weak, lazy and ineffective. Dangerous even.

And yet... and yet, I'm increasingly learning those parts might be misinformed.

When I can welcome myself – even the darkest, ugliest parts of myself - I create space to respond with grace and compassion. It doesn't mean I acquiesce or give up. For me, it means I am orienting to reality as it is. It means I stop fighting reality. I stop battling upstream and instead work with what is actually here. I start from where I am.

I can acknowledge how these parts came to be and how they've served me. And I can choose to learn a new strategy. Because there is no right way to be.

The more range I have, the more choices I have. I can respond to life intelligently, meeting each moment in a way that honours self and honours others. I live authentically.

And it turns out that's powerful. I have so much more energy when I stop battling myself. Most of the things I don't like aren't nearly as terrible as I thought they were when I turn towards them instead of pushing them into the shadows, where they look even more like monsters.

> *"... the curious paradox is that when I accept myself as I am, then I change."*
> *~ Carl Rogers*

Back to my practice. I chose yin yoga with the intention of finding more compassion and acceptance in the face of challenges. I wanted to practise leaning back from my edge, rather than constantly pushing myself to and beyond it.

Something fundamental shifted for me.

Last year, for the first time in five years, I didn't do any new training courses. I gave myself time off from being a constant beginner (and always feeling not good enough) and I allowed myself time to integrate and deepen my practices.

It was a breath of fresh air.

There are still lots of things I want to learn. I still see old patterns show up that I'd like to let go of. The difference is that I don't feel any pressure to do so.

I am complete and I am not finished.

I can follow my heart and soul's desire; I feel drawn to things as opposed to feeling the whip of my own self-brutalisation. I can relax into learning and change. And, funnily enough, change is so much easier when my body is open to receiving it.

It's Not *The Thing*, It's Your Relationship To *The Thing*

"When you are distressed by an external thing, it's not the thing itself that troubles you, but only your judgment of it. And you can wipe this out at a moment's notice."
~ Marcus Aurelius

So often in life, we focus on the object of our attention. We get caught up in the "what". It's all about the thing.

If there's a problem, it's a problem with *the thing*. *The thing* must change for us to feel how we want.

The most common argument my partner and I have at the moment (and this is so silly) is what to have for dinner. The problem is that neither one of us wants to make a decision when we're tired and hungry. The problem is *the thing* we're arguing about.

I had a very challenging experience doing an exercise on my Menstruality Leadership course with Red School.[9] I wasn't having the experience I wanted to have, or thought I should be having. The problem was the exercise – *the thing*.

---

[9] https://www.redschool.net/

I have clients who come to me feeling stuck. Feeling stuck doing too much. Feeling stuck procrastinating about all the things they should be doing. Overthinking decisions and second-guessing themselves. The problem, obviously, is them and their perfectionism and "everything would be fine if only they weren't like this". The problem is *the thing*.

Except it's not.

It's not *the thing*; it's our relationship to *the thing*. We focus on content, not process; what, not how.

Our relationship to *the thing* is our thoughts and feelings about it, how they influence our perception of *the thing*, and ultimately what we decide to do (or not) in response.

We rarely stand back to reflect on our relationship with *the thing* because we're so caught up in it. That's not a failing – that's our nervous systems very sensibly focusing on what looks like a threat.

It's also not that helpful in the long run.

Because we can rarely change *the thing*. I can't make my partner decide what he wants to eat or be better at making decisions. I can't change the course exercise I was asked to do. I can't wave a magic wand and suddenly be a different person with a whole different life experience that doesn't involve perfectionism.

The only thing I can change is how I'm in relationship with *the thing*.

Do I resist it? Do I try to change reality with the sheer force of my willpower?

Or do I surrender? Do I let go of the need to have a perfect experience? Can I allow myself to forget what it "should" be like and be with what is? Can I stay with myself no matter what?

Facing reality and being with it is where our power lies.

Here, I can encounter life with grace. I can accept and welcome everything, trusting that it is already meaningful. I can choose how I'm in relationship with *the thing* and the people around me.

This doesn't mean I have to accept or tolerate the thing, especially if it's harmful. My choice might be to speak out, to stand up for myself, or to walk away from a situation or relationship. And there is rarely a right answer here.

This is not some vague neo-spiritual advice to be all love and light - quite the opposite, in my experience. Facing reality as it is, rather than how I want it to be, helps me make more informed, more effective decisions about how to respond.

That said, I can choose to be kind and patient with my partner and myself. We can have the same disagreements and I can listen to what is being said; we both want to be taken care of. We can develop better habits around meal planning and try not to go too long without a snack (yep, we're basically overgrown toddlers).

In the Menstruality Leadership exercise, I chose to stay with my experience. I remained present to what was happening inside me, embracing the frustration and disappointment. In doing so, something did start to shift and I found myself learning some powerful lessons about myself in the process.

As perfectionists, we can choose not to see ourselves as the problem. The problem isn't perfectionism, per se; "the problem" is that we see our perfectionist selves as a problem to be fixed. Reflecting on our relationship with perfectionism creates a space for us to choose radical self-compassion instead of self-brutalisation. We can learn to work with ourselves, rather than fight against this part of us.

Next time you find yourself in some sort of conflict, whether with yourself or another person or life itself, can you find a way to take a step back? Can you separate the "what" from the "how", the content from the process, and the thing from your relationship to it? And in doing so, maybe you can transform conflict into greater depth and intimacy.

The Power of Appreciation

*"Imperfection inspires invention, imagination, creativity.
It stimulates. The more I feel imperfect, the more I feel alive."
~ Jhumpa Lahiri*

Have you ever thought that perfectionism, overdoing or overthinking are problems you need to overcome or beat? Maybe you thought that life would just work the way you want it to, if only you weren't plagued by such character flaws.

Me too.

The thing is, I realised that this way of thinking is perfectionism in action. Its essence is that there is something wrong with you and you need to be better.

Perfectionism, in all its flavours, is not a character flaw. It's a survival strategy.

It's how your nervous system developed to keep you safe. And may I say, it's done a spectacular job. Not only are you still here but I imagine you've managed to do a whole bunch of impressive things in your life.

Still, I believe that perfectionism is ultimately a maladaptive strategy, one that has served a purpose albeit at a high price.

It's an exhausting and perpetually disappointing way to live: the work is never good enough, the job is never done and there is always room for improvement.

There's something of a paradox here. Approaching perfectionism as a problem that needs to be fixed simply perpetuates it. Yet, I don't want to keep running this old pattern because I can see and feel the limitations of this old survival strategy. Instead, I want to be able to show up as the 30-something adult I am, not the 6-year-old who needed this protection. If I want that choice, I need more options.

Unlearning perfectionism starts with appreciating it.

If we don't take time to acknowledge everything our perfectionism has done for us, those perfectionist parts assume we don't really know how scary the world is and how much we need them to protect us. By appreciating how perfectionism has kept us safe, we can start to create the space for something new.

Perfectionism never really goes away. That pattern of being will always be there somewhere, buried in our neural pathways. And that's okay. We can learn to be compassionate towards it, towards ourselves, as we appreciate that nothing needs to change. Nothing is broken, no one needs fixing. We are already whole and complete.

Someone asked me recently how to move past perfectionism. My answer is I don't think you do; I think you learn to be with it in a different way. You learn to regulate your nervous system to create more safety in your body. You redesign your relationship with your inner critic so it becomes an ally. You learn to work with your cycles, rather than against them, then you can flow with your patterns of energy. You develop your somatic intelligence so you can tap into your body's wisdom and express yourself authentically.

My experience of this work, in myself and my clients, is that this is not easy, yet it is incredibly satisfying. And it starts with showing yourself and your perfectionism a little bit of gratitude for getting you this far.

It seems to me that perfectionism is often driven by scarcity and dissatisfaction. When I'm in perfectionist mode, nothing is quite good enough. So I love the feeling of appreciation as an antidote to the shame and fear of the not-good-enough-ness.

It could be as simple as a Ta-Dah! list. At the end of a busy day, I write down all of the things I did, no matter how small or seemingly insignificant. Seeing all my achievements down on paper never fails to make me appreciate how much I am capable of doing, even on the days when I feel like I've got nothing done.

I still do a little happy dance every time someone signs up to work with me!

It almost feels trite to mention the Japanese art of kintsugi, an exemplification of the spirit of wabi-sabi; it's in danger of becoming an overused metaphor. But there is something I find so soothing and joyful about finding the beauty in imperfection and impermanence – the cracks and brokenness are the opportunity to add in something precious and create something new, something even more beautiful than before. Maybe my imperfection and my humanity aren't just something to be tolerated but something to be celebrated and enjoyed.

As the poet and songwriter, Leonard Cohen said,

"Forget your perfect offering.
There is a crack in everything.
That's how the light gets in."

Stop Trying So Hard

"True discipline is really just self-remembering;
no forcing or fighting is necessary."
~ Charles Eisenstein

Discipline is fundamentally misconstrued, especially by perfectionists and overachievers.

We've learnt that discipline means gritting our teeth and pushing ourselves through adversity. We've been taught that discipline is the opposite of rest; those who lack discipline are weak and lazy. We should ignore our feelings and bodies to keep powering through. We punish and brutalise ourselves to work harder and achieve.

Through this disciplinarian lens, we beat ourselves up for not doing more, taking a break, or voicing doubts. We tell ourselves that we're inferior, imagining that we could have been stronger, more disciplined, and more focused.

There is a time and a place for this kind of discipline. This is what I learned during basic training when I joined the military. I was trained to be able to keep doing my job under enemy fire when lives were literally on the line.

Discipline like this, out of context, led me to burnout some years later. It is neither appropriate nor necessary for the vast majority of us who aren't soldiers, emergency workers or Formula One engineers. And even those people don't need this kind of discipline most of the time.

Discipline, however, is a fundamental skill for anyone who wants to get anything done in this world. It's the structure and order we need for perseverance, consistency, and building new habits.

The most common reason I see coaching clients "fail" is because they don't have the discipline to follow through on the actions they know will get them from A to B. There are times we need to do hard things and discipline helps us do hard things.

How then to be disciplined without being brutal, rigid and inflexible? How to have structure without being ruled by it? How do you stay focused and open at the same time?

This is the paradox at the heart of discipline for creative purposes.

In doing something different to what we've done before, we need to break the rules. We can't keep doing things the same way and expect to get different outcomes.

Yet, at the same time, we need structure in our lives otherwise the only thing we'll ever do is dream.

Jocelyn K. Glei, the host of the Hurry Slowly podcast, calls this tender discipline.[10] Authentic Business coach George Kao calls it structured flow.[11] I like the oxymorons; they embrace the polarities of gentleness and structure.

---

[10] https://hurryslowly.co/215-jocelyn-k-glei/

[11] https://www.georgekao.com/blog/scheduledflow

Tender discipline, as I see it, is a practice of coming into alignment with ourselves rather than forcing ourselves into a box designed by someone else. It's about working with our strengths and weaknesses. Trusting that we innately have the strength and motivation to get things done when we align our actions with our values and intrinsic definitions of success, we do not need to then shame ourselves into action.

Tender discipline is about opening up to possibilities, rather than clamping down. It's a deep "yes" to ourselves. When we are connected to our burning desires, we can kindly and unapologetically say no to everything else – the distractions, the temptations, and the interruptions.

At its heart, it's an invitation to be present and engage in tasks with intention and attention.

This approach allows for structure and spontaneity, holding both as equally important. Being devotional in the time you create for yourself, without committing to a specific task, so your focus is to keep showing up at the same time regardless of the outcomes. Alternatively, commit deeply to a task while allowing yourself the freedom to do it whenever you want.

In my own life, the structure might look like Meeting-Free Mondays – I simply don't say yes to meetings on Mondays (99% of the time!) because I'm often full of energy at the start of the week and I want to use that renewed focus and creativity on the things that matter most to me. I also schedule my period in my diary so I can make sure I'm taking time off to rest following my menstrual cycle.

Other times, I follow my intuition. Maybe I got up early and went for a run, full of beans. But when I sat down to start working, everything felt sticky and awkward; my body felt uncomfortable. So I might take a break before I even get started. Not so long ago, when this happened, I spent an hour in the hammock, chilling out and practising my Indonesian vocab. Then, when I started to get fidgety again (and my husband wouldn't let me annoy him) I decided to open up the laptop again and I felt a sense of flow and ease.

Ultimately, tender discipline is a practice that prioritises our nervous system regulation. It knows that stress makes us less smart, less creative and less kind. It's a way of working that supports our efforts from our bodies up.

It invites us to be gentle and graceful with ourselves. To release ourselves from the incessant pressure we put ourselves under. To gift ourselves the space to flourish, feel, and flow.

Focus on how

Tender discipline concerns itself with the act over the outcome. The how, the quality of our time, becomes the focus of our attention.

Instead of focusing on what we want to do, we can switch our focus to how we want to feel.

- add adverbs to your to-do list e.g. joyfully write a newsletter, cheerfully call Jamie, attentively reconcile the accounts;
- ask yourself, "what would 1% more ease/fun/focus feel like?"
- connect to the "why" of your goals, so you can hold the outcome lightly

Embrace your own rhythm

Productivity isn't a state we can enter on demand; there's no on-switch. Instead, we all have different cycles of when we function best. Rather than resist what our bodies are doing anyway, we can work with them and they will be our allies.

If I had to sum up the benefit of practising cyclical wisdom in one sentence, it would be "there is a right time for everything".

Cyclical living – being more in tune and attentive to my rhythms – has been a permission slip to rest when I need to and to be all-in at those times when my energy is high and I could conquer worlds.

- schedule breaks and time to rest at times that work for your body;
- prioritise momentum and follow your natural flow of energy;
- plan with your most productive and least productive selves in mind; learn your cycles.

Be on your tender edge

If this is new to you, tender discipline can feel clumsy or slow. Growth inherently feels awkward and challenging. Practising tender discipline won't always feel "good"; unfamiliar is often uncomfortable. It will feel "right" somewhere in your system – perhaps a sense of relief, like finding an oasis in the desert or a deep sigh. It's effective action without forcing or straining.

- learn what "right" feels like in your body by experimenting – for example, how does it feel to run when you're energised and well-rested, compared to a day when you push yourself beyond your limits?

- be patient; it will take time for this to become familiar;
- our souls need growth and our nervous systems need safety; if in doubt, prioritise resourcing your nervous system because you can't learn or be creative if you're triggered.

Authenticity Over Perfection

"I'm never more courageous than when I'm embracing imperfection, embracing vulnerabilities, and setting boundaries with the people in my life."
~ Brené Brown

One way perfectionism shows up for me is the "I'm worried I'm not good enough and everyone will find out" problem, otherwise known as imposter syndrome.

Perfectionism is my armour. It's the mask I wear to protect myself and make sure I'm acceptable to others.

Right at the heart of perfectionism, there's shame. As Brene Brown describes, we then carry around this twenty-ton shield hoping to protect ourselves but all we end up doing is isolating ourselves from the world. We desperately want to be accepted for who we are and yet we rarely allow the world to see us that way.

Perfectionism is a trap that authenticity can open.

Perfectionism is fear. Fear of not being enough. Fear of being rejected for who we are. Fear of being the only one who's still figuring it out and f**king it up.

Perfectionism is fear and authenticity is courage.

It's the courage to let go of what others think, celebrate our quirks, and welcome our imperfections. It's brave to allow ourselves to be vulnerable and to be fully seen by others. Hell, it takes guts to drop out of our heads and feel our bodies, hear our heartbeats, and connect with our intuition – because what if it says something you don't want to hear?!

Authenticity is freedom.

And it starts with dropping the armour and revealing ourselves, allowing ourselves to be seen.

Revealing your experience is an invitation for people to join you in your world, exactly as it is. It's a practice of making the hidden seen, the implicit explicit, and the unconscious conscious. Revealing my experience to myself, and then to others, builds on the practices of awareness and acceptance to say "this is me, right now, in all my humanity, strength and vulnerability".

This is not easy. There is a part of me that is terrified of revealing myself in case I'm rejected. But the irony is that I'm rejecting myself when I don't admit my truth. So I lose either way.

But when I lean into that vulnerability, when I take that risk, I never fail to have the sense that it's okay. That I don't need that other person to approve of me because I'm okay with who I am – I'm standing by myself.

Now, not everyone will get this. There will be people who tell you that you shouldn't feel that way or who will try to 'fix' you. That is not your problem. Most likely, that person is deeply uncomfortable with those aspects and feelings inside themselves and they don't know how to deal with it. You do not need to be fixed, you are not broken, and it's absolutely okay that you feel that way.

More often though, the experience I have when I reveal myself is warmth and open-heartedness. I know I love it when someone allows me to see them – it brings me so much joy to witness the aliveness in another person, no matter what flavour of aliveness that is.

And nine times out of ten, I have a "me too" moment. I realise that I am not alone in my experience. It's not just me. I'm not broken or messed up or doing it wrong because this other human can relate to my experience. It turns out we're all just humaning along together. The danger of silence and keeping it all in is that we start to believe we're alone and we're really not.

What Self-Care Really Means

*"Selfish is caring for ourselves at others' expense.
Self-care is taking care of ourselves so that we can
be there for others."*
~ Bill Crawford

Human beings aren't meant to operate like machines — at high speeds, continuously, for long periods. We have natural rhythms that influence our energy throughout the day and the year. We must balance the mental, physical, creative, social and spiritual aspects of our lives. When we make time for reflection and rest, we can look after our bodies, our minds, our environments, and our souls. This is the key to cultivating a sense of purpose and autonomy we need to thrive.

When we work with our natural rhythms – the natural ebb and flow of our energy – we create more energy, not less. When we step into our authenticity and dare to be our full selves, we stop wasting energy lugging around all the heavy armour that is perfectionism.

This is a radical form of self-compassion and it looks quite different from the Instagram version of self-care.

For us busy overachievers, self-care can so easily become another thing on our increasingly long to-do lists. As if it's a single task that we can simply tick off on our way to productivity nirvana.

The problem with this is that self-care is not prescriptive. At its best, it's responsive to how we feel, where we are in our cycles, and the environment around us. It's the difference between the answers to the question "are you taking care of yourself?" (hopefully yes) and "how are you taking care of yourself?".

Force-marching yourself to a bubble bath because you 'should' be practising self-care is as much use as a chocolate teapot.

Stripped down, self-care means noticing how you are and meeting yourself there. When you tune into yourself, you see that your needs change from day to day, from month to month. Making a habit of checking in with yourself makes you more aware of your own needs, which in turn helps you cultivate the practices you need to rejuvenate yourself, day in and day out.

Self-care means you prioritise your relationship with yourself before anyone else. It is impossible to connect or take care of anyone else if you are not first in connection with yourself – the old adage of putting your own oxygen mask on first. It's the difference between being responsible for everything and everyone – the people-pleasing aspect of perfectionism – and being 'response-able', able to be sensitive and responsive to yourself, others and a situation rather than being reactive.

It takes intentional effort to sustain any relationship, especially one many of us are so used to putting last. It's not always glamorous or relaxing. Sometimes self-care means calling yourself out on the things you're doing that aren't healthy for you. Sometimes it means getting out of our own way, even if it's deeply uncomfortable.

Sometimes, self-care is less about bubble baths and journaling and more about doing the hard work of saying no and setting boundaries.

Self-care requires work that looks a little different for everyone. It can look like:

- admitting that you don't want to do it all by yourself and allowing yourself to accept help;
- setting boundaries and saying no to requests you aren't comfortable with or invitations that you feel you 'should' accept;
- saying yes to new experiences and expanding your comfort zone;
- replacing toxic habits with healthier coping mechanisms, like meditation or exercise;
- letting yourself eat an entire tub of ice cream without feeling bad about it;
- choosing eight hours' sleep over watching another episode on Netflix;
- watching another episode on Netflix instead of getting eight hours' sleep.

All, some or none of these things might work for you — what matters is focusing on what feels right for your needs.

Here's a quick and simple audit you can do to make sure you're caring for yourself and meeting your needs.

1. Write a list of things that energise, nourish and relax you.
2. Write another list of things that deplete and drain you or bring you down.
3. Do more of the first list and less of the second.

I told you it was quick and simple – we perfectionists do like to overcomplicate things sometimes.

My lists look something like this at the moment:

Things that lift me up

- Playing authentic relating games;
- Exercising (and I have to remember I feel this after exercising not before!);
- Crossing things off my to-do list;
- A cup of tea (seriously, never fails).

Things that bring me down

- Not getting enough sleep;
- Trying to decide what to eat when I'm hungry (hello, meal planning!);
- Bingeing Netflix to avoid facing tension with my partner;
- Anything with a sentence that starts with "I should..."

Self-care is how you fuel yourself on your journey to redesign your relationship with perfectionism. That change doesn't happen overnight, and caring for yourself in the process might be the most radical thing you can do.

A Pause to Reflect

What do your lists look like and how could you do a little more of the first and a little less of the second?

Conclusion: Doing Perfectionist While Writing a Book About Perfectionism

I'm a recovering perfectionist writing a book about perfectionism and enoughness, whilst dealing with my own perfectionist flare-up. That irony is not lost on me.

More and more, I realise my perfectionism kicks in when I'm attempting something new. It's a familiar companion every time I step beyond the edges of my comfort zone, including in the writing of this book.

It first showed up in deciding on the theme of the book. Of all the things I could write about, what would be the 'right' one? It reared its head again in deciding when to stop writing with the all too familiar question of "is this enough?"

Choosing the 'right' title was a small ordeal. I found myself caught between the popular option, that everyone said was the right way to go, and what felt authentic to me and my voice. As someone who spends a lot of time talking about authenticity and following your somatic intuition, I found it disconcertingly hard to honour mine. That's what perfectionism does; it pits my head against my heart and convinces me that everyone else must know more than me.

Perfectionism is my system's response to uncertainty and unpredictability. My perfectionism hates there not being a wrong answer. Because if there is no wrong answer, how will I know I picked the right one?

This book became another opportunity to encounter my perfectionism and to choose the path of tenderness and self-compassion instead of self-brutality.

Every time I felt resistance or discomfort, I had to discern whether my perfectionism had snuck through the back door and, once again, was masquerading as wanting to do a good job. That wasn't easy; my perfectionism does a wonderful job of pretending to be benign.

What I'm realising is that if I even need to ask the question, there is almost certainly some kind of perfectionism involved, no matter how much I try to tell myself there isn't. If in doubt, assume it's perfectionism!

Self-awareness is necessary and not sufficient. Recognising my perfectionism without having the tools to respond differently is perhaps even worse than not noticing it in the first place.

And so, I've done my best throughout this process to practice what I preach.

I asked for help. I reached out to peers, colleagues and mentors for support. I chose to reveal my vulnerability instead of trying to figure everything out on my own. Every single time I did, I was met with care, perspective and a whole squad of cheerleaders. It still amazes me how supportive other people want to be when I let them in.

I also had to give myself permission, with the support of my mentor, to take this process at my own pace. I found the right balance of discipline and flow for me, sensitive to my rhythms and needs. The right kind of external accountability also helped here; knowing my editors were expecting a draft gave me the nudge I needed to keep moving forward, even when it felt out of reach.

This brings me to a piece of advice my mother has been repeating for as long as I can remember:

"The best way to eat an elephant is one bite at a time."

I can so easily derail myself by worrying about step 57 before I've taken the first step – classic control freak and over-doer. Remembering to take one step at a time and to keep making those steps as small as possible – in this case, taking it one chapter or even one paragraph at a time – has kept me gently moving forward.

Until I was ready to stop. Part of me wanted to keep adding more and more content to this book, desperately wanting to make sure it was good enough – not for the first time, mistaking 'more' for 'better'. In the end, I decided to be brave and let this be enough. Discerning 'enough' is one of the hardest lessons I'm learning as a recovering perfectionist; my new rule of thumb is that enough is always a little bit less than I'm inclined to think it is.

Even then, it took a blog post from Seth Godin on getting stuck on titles to give me permission to go with the title I wanted. And it was only in adding this experience to this closing chapter that I re-read these words and felt myself come full circle. *Enough* is enough.

Unlearning a lifetime of perfectionism doesn't happen overnight. Perfectionist thinking would have us believe that the goal is to never experience perfectionism again. The true art is to notice perfectionist tendencies more quickly, be sensitive to their increasing subtlety, and respond with more grace and compassion.

My hope is that you've received something from this book that might help you encounter yourself more tenderly. If you're feeling ready to finally transform your relationship with needing to get it right, you can find free tools to help you take the next step at www.vixanderton.com/links.

One of the strange things about writing a book---instead of having a conversation---is that I don't know the person I'm 'talking' to through this book. And I would love to get to know you, so please send me an email at vix@vixanderton.com and say hi.

With grace and gratitude,

Can you help by adding a review?

If you enjoyed the book and believe that it could serve others, there's a tangible way to help with that: leave a book review.

Every review does help more people find this book.

It can be short; 1-2 sentences are enough. It gives a potential reader a bit more confidence that it would be worthwhile to read the book.

1. Go to http://www.Amazon.com

2. Search for this book's title, and click to go to the book's page.

3. Click on "Write a review". It doesn't have to be long.
Consider briefly answering these questions:

- What type of person would you recommend this book to?
- What did you love about this book?
- Is there another book (or resource) that people might also enjoy, in conjunction with this book? Let's share the love!

Surprisingly few readers (of any book) take the time to leave a review. You'll be making a real difference if you do.

Thank you,
Vix

Acknowledgements

Five wonderful friends and clients read the manuscript and gave me thoughtful feedback (and a lot of cheerleading).

Chris Kenworthy – https://www.chriskenworthy.co.uk/
Debbie Lee – https://www.debbielee.co.uk/
Gabe De Rita – https://effectiveconnection.com/
Jacqueline Hill – https://www.jhillassociates.co.uk/
Samantha Arter

Thank you for your time, your patience, your eye for detail and your support.

While this book reflects much of my journey with perfectionism, it wouldn't have been possible without the clients I have had the privilege to work with over the past five years. Thank you for your trust. I honour your willingness to grow and challenge your status quo. It's been my pleasure to walk alongside you.

Thank you to my fellow recovering perfectionists who have taken the time to share their experiences of perfectionism with me. You've deepened my understanding of perfectionism and this book is all the richer for your voices.

Thank you to everyone who reads my posts. Every time I see your likes, comments and replies, I light up. I'm touched by the moments of resonance and I realise that I'm not alone on this journey.

There's no such thing as an original idea and my work is no different. I have been fortunate to study with and learn from some incredible teachers, who have influenced my approach and I would like to credit them here.

My embodiment teachers, Mark Walsh, Rachel Blackman, Karin van Maanen, and the rest of the Embodied Facilitator Course community.

My Authentic Relating teachers, Ryel Kestano, Jason Digges, Rick Smith, Dayna Seraye and the team at ART International.

My menstruality teachers, Alexandra Pope and Sjanie Hugo Wurlizter and the community at Red School.

My business mentors Tad Hargrave, George Kao and Caroline Leon who have helped me learn ways of building a business that don't feel icky or incongruent. It was George's From Blog to Book course that inspired me to finally write this book.

I've also been influenced by the work of Irene Lyon, Ginny Whitelaw, Paul Linden, Richard Strozzi-Heckler, Philip Shepherd, Lisa Feldman Barrett, Amanda Blake, Susan David, Brene Brown, Elizabeth Gilbert, Steven Covey, James Hollis, Gay Hendricks, Michael Neil, Daniel Goleman, David Treleaven and so many more.

Last, but by no means least, my heartfelt gratitude to my husband and my family. No matter where I go in the world, I know that you are always there for me. Thank you for helping shape me into the person who could write this book.

About The Author

Vix Anderton is a perfectionism and productivity coach for chronic over-doers, overthinkers and stressed-out control freaks. She helps them turn their inner critic into an ally and find powerful and sustainable ways to get on with what they care about without overwhelm and burnout.

Vix served in the Royal Air Force for 10 years before entering the international development sector. With her experience in high-stress environments from war zones to boardrooms and a resulting burnout, she is now committed to helping other recovering perfectionists learn how they can manage their energy and emotions and reconnect with their natural flow, intelligence and creativity, thus enabling them to build more sustainable and authentic ways of being.

Enough: An Imperfect Antidote to Perfectionism is Vix's first book. In it, she takes the view that perfectionism isn't the character flaw we've been led to believe, rather it's a strategy we use to feel safe albeit one that comes at a high cost. She lays out an alternative approach to redesigning our relationship with perfectionism to feel deeply enough as we are.

Having lived in as many houses as years she has been alive, Vix is now settling on the Indonesian Island of Bali with her husband and 3 rescue kittens. She can be found at Ecstatic Dance, learning to hula-hoop or enjoying one of Ubud's many vegan cafes.

Vix offers coaching and online courses for recovering perfectionists. You can find all her current programmes at www.vixanderton.com.

For free embodied and authentic strategies to rebel against the status quo, define success on your terms and reconnect with your natural flow, intelligence and creativity, visit www.vixanderton.com/enough.

Printed in Great Britain
by Amazon